New Beginnings:

Refugee Children's Tales of Hope and Resilience

Carter T. Magnano & Sarah C. Park

AUTHORS

Carter Magnano

A senior at Ponte Vedra High School, is co-president of JaxTHRIVE, and has been a dedicated tutor for the past seven years. He is grateful for the unique opportunity to witness JaxTHRIVE's impressive growth in both size and impact. Last year, he was excited to successfully launch their popular virtual SAT and ACT test preparation program. Carter also co-founded SmartART, an art appreciation program that enriches the lives of senior assisted living residents, memory care patients, and homeless families through creative expression and community engagement. Carter has demonstrated his leadership skills in various roles, serving as president of both his elementary and middle schools, and as a Student Council Representative at Ponte Vedra High School. He is a National Honor Society Board member and is a graduate of the Youth Leadership Jacksonville program, a OneJax Metrotown Ambassador and LOUD Leader, and he has been a significant contributor to the Ponte Vedra High School varsity lacrosse team. These experiences have helped him embrace diversity, collaborate with others, and assume larger leadership roles in different aspects of his life.

.

Sarah Park

A senior at the Bolles School, is co-president of JaxTHRIVE and has been a volunteer since her 6th grade, building relationships with refugee students, mentoring both in-person and virtually, and helping them adjust and succeed academically. She has dedicated her time to involving refugee students in STEM literacy through hands-on science projects. Sarah is an active scientist, musician, and community advocate. She was named 2021 3M America's Top Young Scientist, earning a $25,000 prize through her passions in science and music. Through her scientific research, she won the 3rd place Grand Award at the '22, '23, and '24 Regeneron International Science and Engineering Fair. She serves as concertmaster in Jacksonville's Symphony Youth Orchestra, sharing her musical talent with the community in schools, churches, nursing homes, and wherever music is needed. Additionally, Sarah founded the Jacksonville chapter of the Back to Bach Project and serves as the regional director, where she and other musicians share classical music with underserved K-12 students, spreading the love of music.

TABLE OF CONTENTS

INTRODUCTION

Many children are born into a cozy home where they feel safe and happy. It's a place where they can grow up and play with their brothers and sisters, parents, friends, classmates and neighbors.

But sometimes, families need to move to find a better place to live and work. Other times, they have to move because of major issues such as war, climate change or other frightening events.

When this happens, children may have to leave everything behind—their favorite toys, books, pets, family and friends.

They will move to a new place that can feel strange and scary, with a different language, culture and customs. Sometimes they can't go to school or play outside in this new environment.

1

Today, more people than ever before have had to leave their homes, and over 43 million of them are children!

Every child should be welcomed and loved.

All children, no matter where they are from or why they had to move, should be treated with kindness and respect.

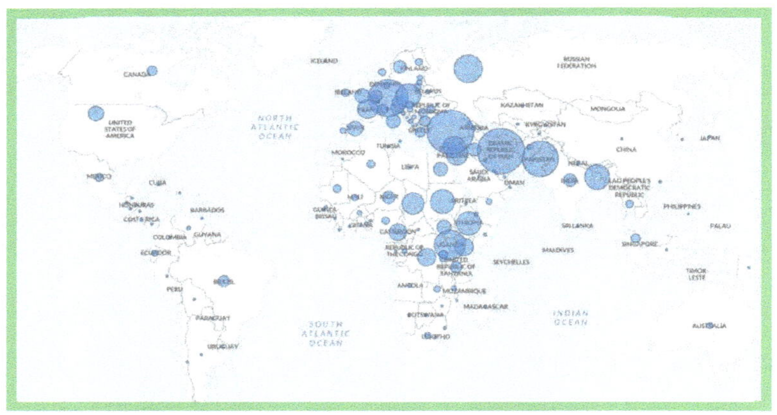

**Map of refugees' countries of origin
(UNHCR)**

*"You have to understand,
no one puts their children in a boat
unless the water is safer than the land."
- Warsan Shire*

2

As you can imagine, education—a fundamental human right—is disrupted for many refugee children. According to the United Nations High Commission for Refugees (UNHCR), 51% of school-aged refugee children worldwide are not enrolled in school. Even those who do attend may find themselves in under-resourced classrooms.

Often, refugee children are placed in classrooms based on their age, which can lead to significant learning gaps. Imagine being placed in a new school in a country where you speak a different language, after not having been in school for months or even years, only to find yourself in a history class with US-born peers. This can be incredibly challenging!

Our goal at JaxTHRIVE, a student-led non-profit organization, is to provide a nurturing and welcoming environment to help refugee students flourish in the community through tutoring, mentorship, and friendship.

Every other Saturday, JaxTHRIVE hosts "Super Saturday", a fun, half-day program where teen volunteers help mentor refugee children. They enjoy activities including reading sessions, STEM projects, art and soccer workshops. Additionally, they host virtual tutoring sessions during the weekdays and a quarterly JaxTHRIVE Journeys interactive lecture series to share the stories, history and culture of their refugee students' homelands.

In this book, we will explore and share the diverse stories of refugee children, which illustrate the values of hope, resilience, determination and friendship.

We hope you enjoy reading these inspirational, real-life stories of our refugee students (*names are changed for the purpose of the book).

Story 1

GALYNA AND SERHII'S BRAVE JOURNEY TO THE UNITED STATES

A story from Ukraine

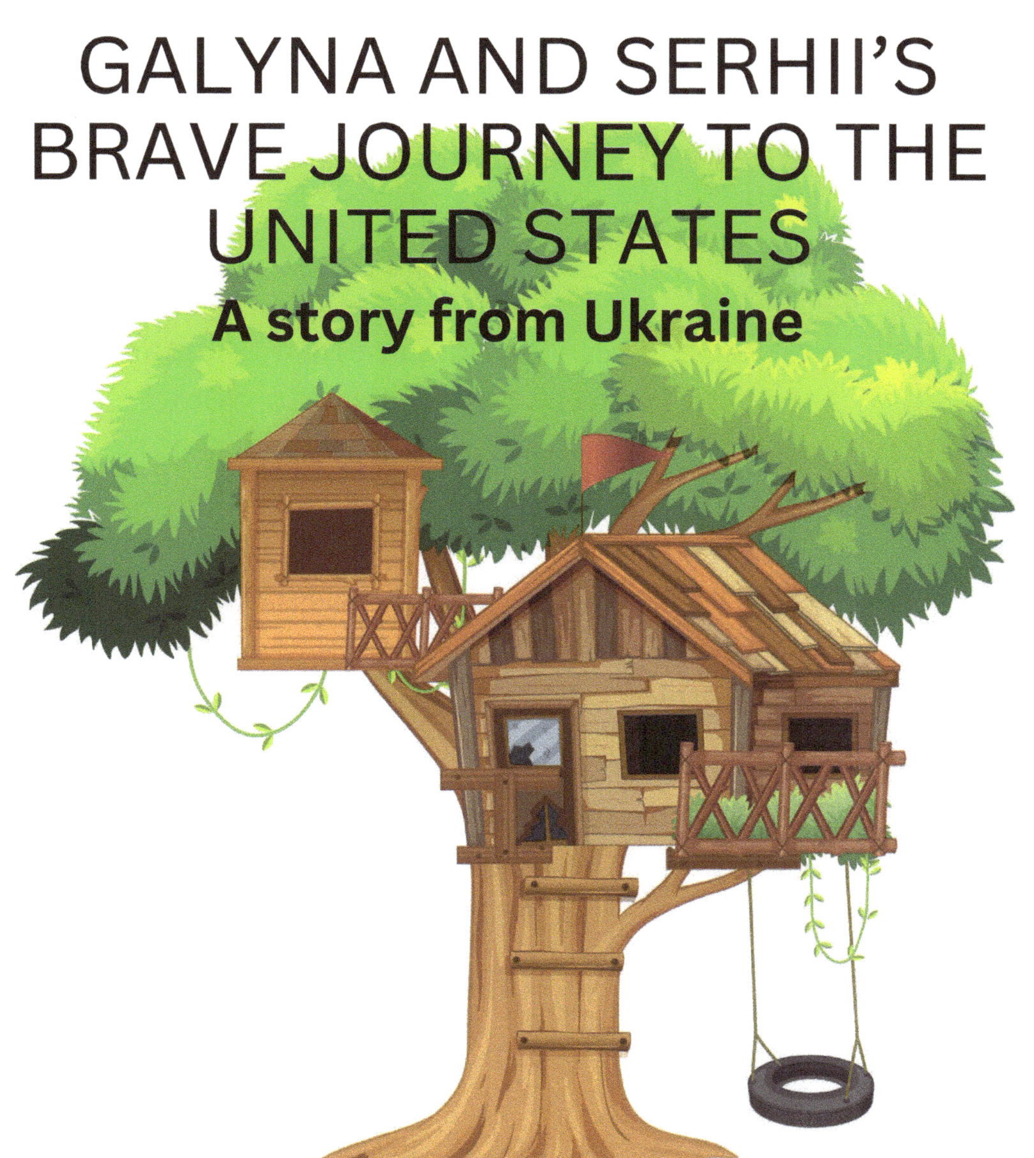

Galyna and Serhii were young children living in southern Ukraine. They loved their home, particularly their playhouse that their father, whom they lovingly called Tato, built for them in their backyard. This wasn't just any playhouse - it was a two-story, magical treehouse! The bottom floor had a sandbox, perfect for building castles and digging for buried treasure. Upstairs was a big room where they could look out over their garden. There was even a super-fast slide that they could whoosh down in a flash!

Galyna and Serhii, along with their friends, spent many happy hours in that treehouse. As the stars came out at night, Tato would light a warm fire in the nearby fire pit. The children would gather around, snuggled in warm blankets, sharing thrilling ghost stories that made their treehouse feel even cozier. In the very early hours of the morning on a quiet, snowy day in February, everything changed for Serhii and Galyna. All of a sudden, loud noises boomed throughout their city—it was the sound of bombs falling.

The two siblings were very scared! Quickly, they gathered their most important things: a few warm sweaters, their three favorite books, important family documents, and Galyna's special traditional Ukrainian pillow that she loved very much.

Their grandmother, whom they called Babousa, had been visiting them. So, all five family members squeezed into their tiny compact car and raced off! Their brave Tato drove as fast as he could toward the safety of the Ukrainian-Polish border. When they arrived, it was time for a very sad goodbye. Their father had to stay behind- it was his duty, and the duty of all Ukrainian men, to protect their homeland.

Before they parted, Tato gave Serhii a Snickers bar, a special treat to remember him by. Serhii treasured that moment so much that he has kept that candy wrapper in a secret box for years! It was a reminder of his father's love and bravery, as Tato continues to fight in the war.

Galyna and Serhii, along with their Mama and Babousa, spent their first two months in a new country living with a kind American family in Krakow, Poland. This family had started a Christian school where the siblings learned new things every day. After two months, once their US visas and travel papers were ready, they said goodbye to Poland and flew to Jacksonville, Florida to start a brand-new chapter of their lives.

When they arrived at the Jacksonville airport, a friendly group from Lutheran Social Services was there with big smiles to welcome them. They helped the family find a cozy apartment where they could all live together.

Starting school in America felt a bit scary at first because they only knew a little English from their lessons back in Ukraine. But it didn't take long for Serhii and Galyna to make new friends and find happiness in their new school.

The siblings learned about JaxTHRIVE, a special program on Saturdays that's designed just for kids like them—children who have come from far away to find a safe place to live.

At JaxTHRIVE, they could learn English, science, art, and even play soccer. Serhii and Galyna were thrilled! They looked forward to Saturday, where they could meet other kids who had similar stories and share their adventures together.

Story 2

AHMAD'S BIRD CATCHING ADVENTURE & BIG DREAM

A story from Afghanistan

Ahmad stood at the edge of the playground in Jacksonville, Florida, watching the other children play with a mix of curiosity and longing. He missed the fields of Afghanistan where he and his cousins chased birds, their laughter filling the air. Three years had passed since Ahmad and his family had left their small town, seeking refuge in the United States. Life here was vastly different, but Ahmad held on to his dreams of one day reuniting his scattered family in a home that he would build himself.

At JaxTHRIVE, a community where Ahmad learns English and makes new friends, he feels like he belongs. He loves sharing stories about his homeland and his exciting bird-catching adventures. Ahmad describes how he would wake up very early and head to the mountains with his father, uncles, and cousins to capture birds. This is an ancient sport in Afghanistan. Together, they would make traditional rectangular bird-catching nets and use them to gently capture birds, placing them carefully into special wooden cages. "We keep the birds as pets, and they bring so much happiness to our family," Ahmad says with a smile.

Ahmad's friends listen eagerly as he shares his dream of becoming an engineer who designs buildings and homes. Their support and interest give him the determination to pursue his goals. Ahmad wants to design a beautiful house where all his relatives can happily live together again.

Each night, Ahmad gazes out at the vast sky, whispering a silent promise to himself. He misses Afghanistan deeply, but he is filled with hope and determination. One day, he will build that house and bring his family together again. Until then, he will take each day as it comes, learning, growing, and working towards his dream, step-by-step, brick-by-brick.

Story 3

BILEN'S GOLDEN TICKET TO THE US!

A story from Eritrea

In 2011, life in Eritrea became very difficult, and many people had to leave their homes. There were several reasons for this, such as their strict government, people not being treated fairly, not having enough money, and not having basic freedoms. These problems made it very hard for families to live happily in Eritrea.

Bilen's family said heartfelt goodbyes to many of their neighbors as things became dangerous in their neighborhood. When bombs started falling too close to their house, Bilen's parents decided it was time to leave. They applied for the US Diversity Visa lottery, which many people call "The Golden Ticket." They knew their chances of winning were slim, but one day, Bilen's parents started jumping up and down with joy—they had actually won the lottery!

Winning "The Golden Ticket" was incredibly exciting, but it meant that they had to go through the detailed process of filling out paperwork and getting ready to move to the United States.

Bilen's family had to leave Eritrea for Ethiopia to start getting everything ready. They needed to prepare important documents, have medical check-ups, and go to visa interviews. After six long years, Bilen's family finally received their visas and were invited to move to the United States.

Bilen remembers her first day in Kindergarten in the United States. She didn't speak or understand any English, which made her first day very challenging. Once, she raised her hand to stretch, but the teacher thought Bilen had a question and called on her. Bilen didn't know how to respond! It was a surprising cultural difference that made her first day of school quite an adventure.

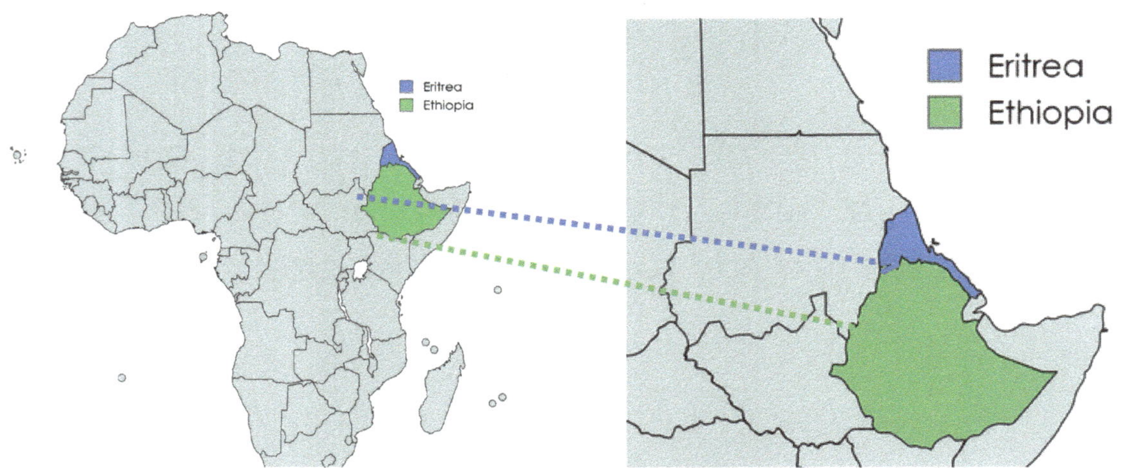

Currently, Bilen is a smart 11-year-old girl in 4th grade who dreams of becoming a doctor. Her father, whom she calls Baba, works as a mechanic, while her mother, whom she calls Ema, cares for their family.

When Bilen and her brother Yonadab learned about the opportunities at JaxTHRIVE, they were excited to join. JaxTHRIVE offered help with learning English and other activities. They have been part of JaxTHRIVE for the past three years, enjoying the Super Saturdays and studying virtually with their friendly tutors.

Story 4

DREAMS ACROSS BORDERS: ONE YOUNG GIRL'S JOURNEY TO LEARN

A story from Afghanistan

In a faraway land called Afghanistan, a young girl named Roya loved learning at her all-girls school, surrounded by her many friends. Each school day started with a long, bumpy, dangerous journey on difficult roads that took over an hour each way. She absolutely loved school, but faced challenges at home. Her aunts and uncles often wondered why Roya continued to study, believing that once a girl learned how to read, she should quit school and help her mother with chores at home.

Yet, Roya's parents believed deeply in the power of education and wanted a better life for their daughter than they had themselves. They dreamed of a much brighter future for Roya.

19

When Roya turned 16, her family made a brave decision to leave everything behind in Afghanistan and move to India to escape the increasing dangers at home. Adapting to her new country in India was hard, especially learning the Hindi language, which was so unfamiliar. While her younger siblings were able to go to school, Roya was considered too old.

Instead, she could only attend an adult part-time school where she studied a few subjects like math and English for just one or two hours each day. But Roya never gave up hope! She studied hard every day on her own, preparing for an important university entrance exam.

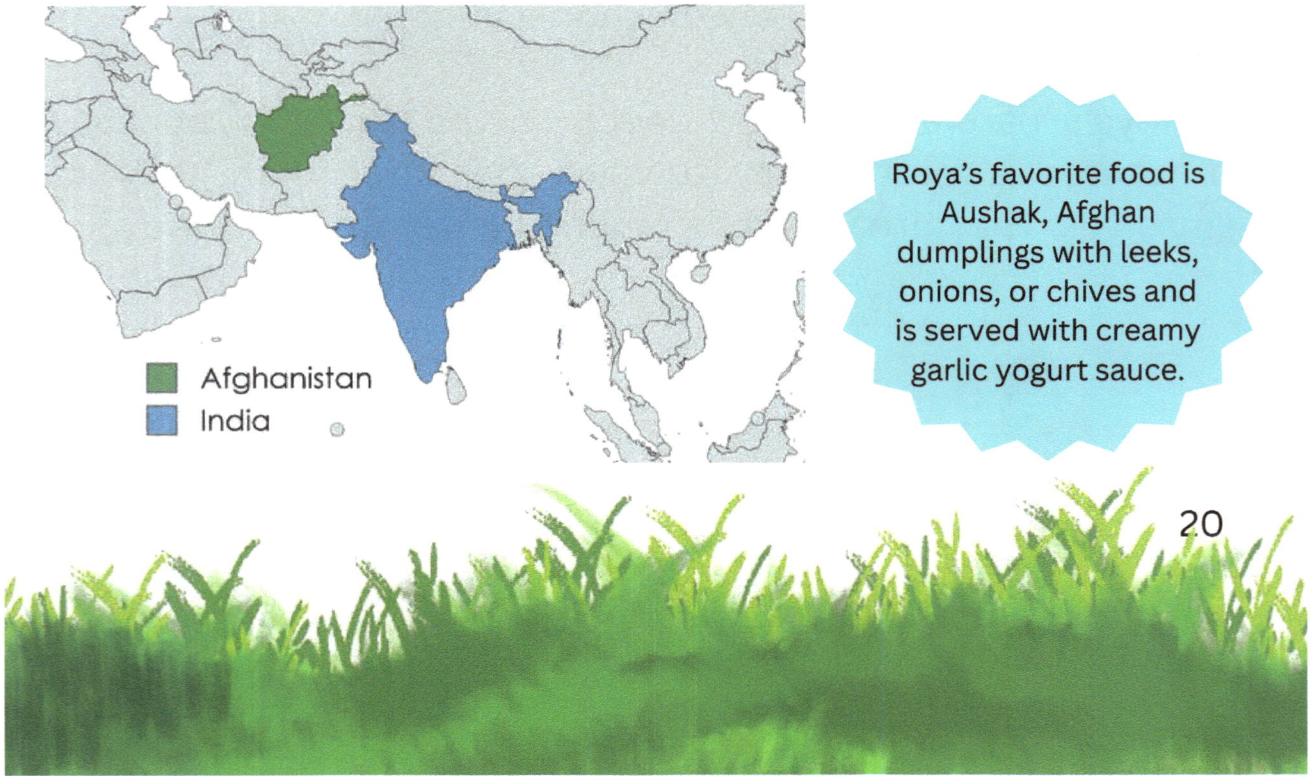

20

Roya's hard work and determination paid off when she passed the exam with flying colors, earning a full scholarship to a highly-regarded virtual university designed especially for displaced students from all over the world. This university was part of a global effort, involving many countries and organizations to help students just like her.

Now in her final year, Roya is thankful for her educational journey, which has brought her closer to achieving her dreams despite her many obstacles. Roya and her family of 7 were recently resettled in her new city of Jacksonville, FL. She is excited to join a program she just learned about called JaxTHRIVE where her whole family can study, meet new friends, and have fun!

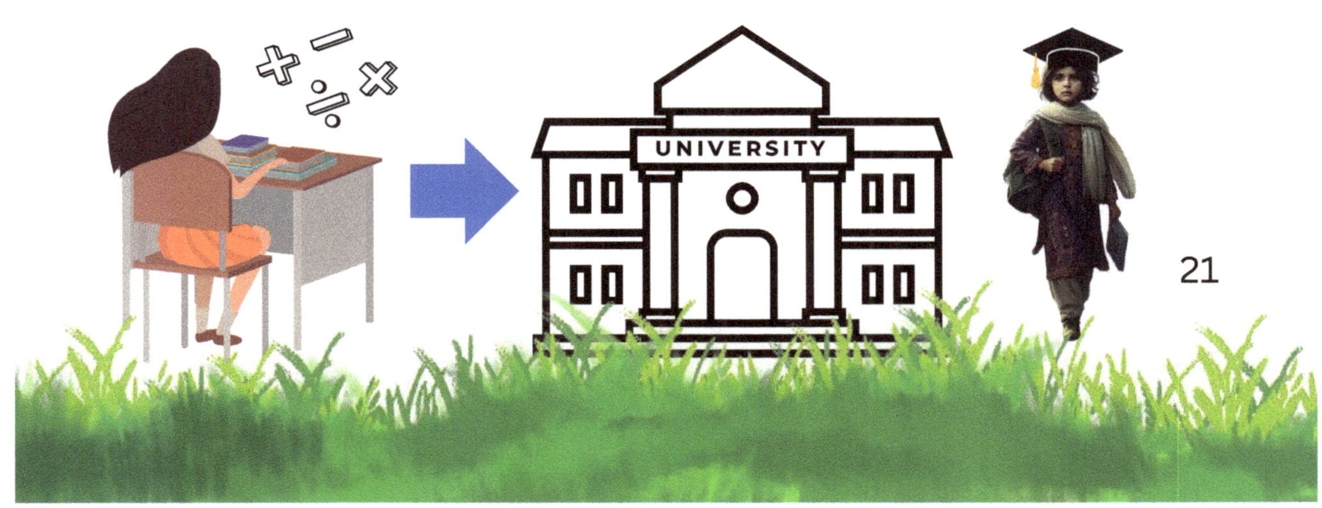

Story 5

Amira's Soaring Dream

A story from Sudan

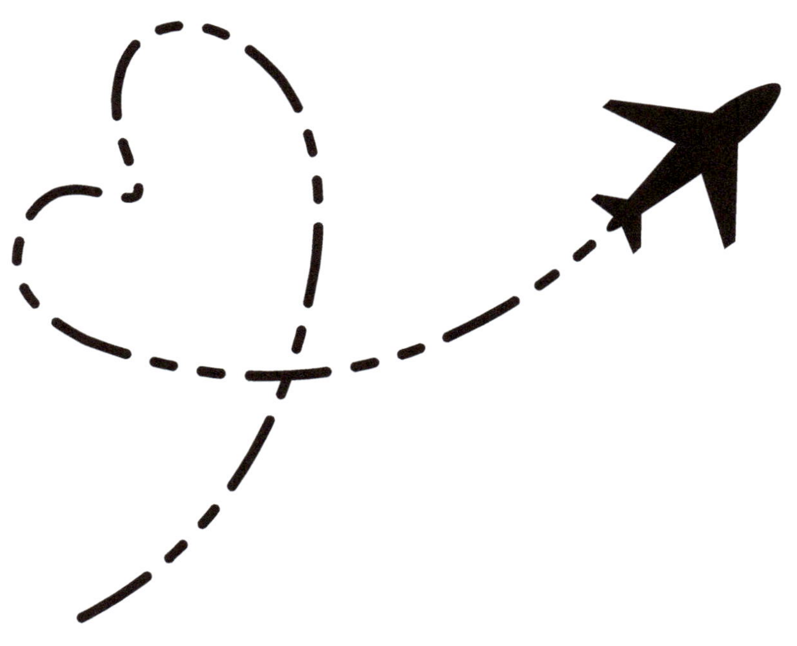

Amira's journey is one of resilience and determination, shaped by the turmoil of her homeland of Darfur which is located in Sudan. Born amidst conflict, she and her family sought refuge in Chad, where her dreams of becoming a pilot began to take flight. Despite the chaos surrounding her, she found comfort in her grandfather's song and the promise of a brighter future.

She said, "My favorite part of fixing my grandpa tea in the morning was hearing him sing songs for me."

O' Amira, the girl who fights for Darfur
Rise once more
Your justice words turn the world around
I beg you, rise again

"Ami" her mother spoke her nickname softly. "I want you to remember your story. You always wanted to obtain a full education so that you could become a pilot and fight for your country. This is a strong goal and I want to let you fly."

She knew her mother was right. In Sudan, girls don't have many opportunities to go to school and pursue careers. By 15 years old, they're expected to be married, have children and raise a family. Neither Amira nor her mother wanted that.

Her journey to America was filled with uncertainty and a longing for stability. Leaving behind her beloved Darfur, she faced many challenges and unexpected detours. Before moving to the US, she spent over a year living in Cameroon while her family prepared their visas and other travel documents. During this time, she couldn't go to school because she wasn't a legal resident of Cameroon.

After one year, with perseverance and the support of her family, Amira finally arrived in Jacksonville, Florida, ready to pursue her dreams.

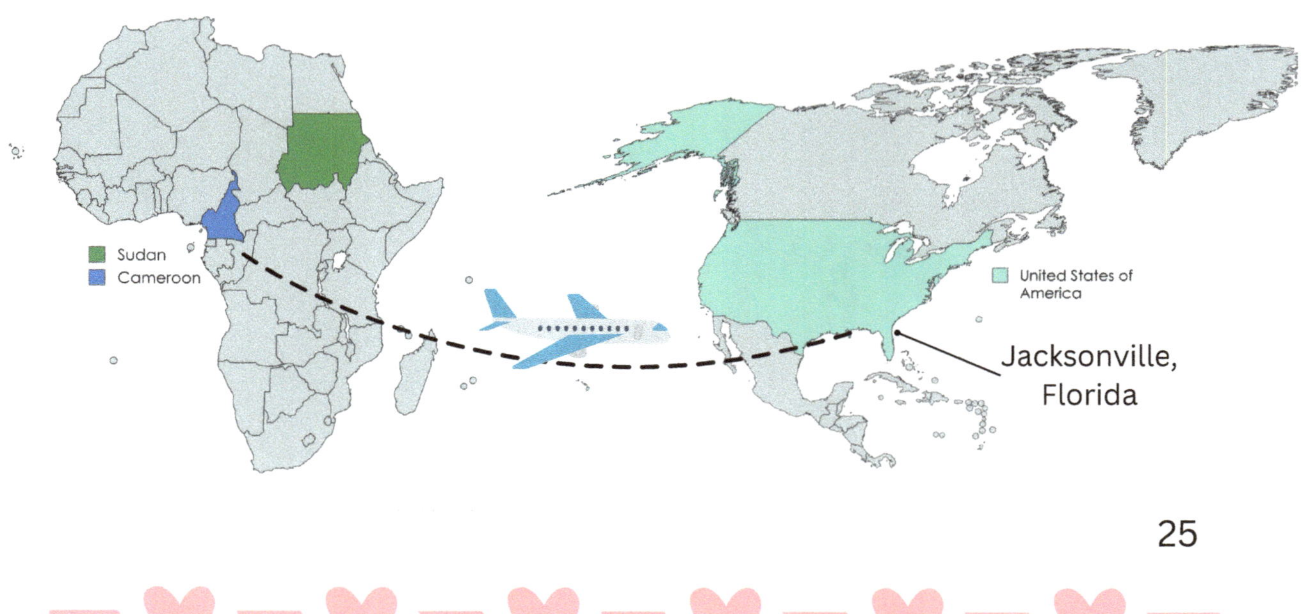

25

Now 18-years-old, Amira is in full pursuit of her new dream as she graduates high school and begins college in Jacksonville.

"Peace in every home, on every street, and in every village of Darfur. This is my dream."

Story 6

THE LOST BOYS OF SUDAN

A story from South Sudan

At just ten years old, Akol's world changed forever. His peaceful village in South Sudan, filled with families, friends and laughter, was suddenly quiet. During a terrible war, his village was destroyed, and he lost his family.

One summer day, Akol and his cousins were spending the day, way up in the mountains, looking after their cattle. When they returned that evening, their homes had burned down and scary soldiers were everywhere. The boys were very frightened, so they ran as fast as they could deep into the forest to hide. They were not wearing any shoes and did not have any food to eat or water to drink.

Soon, Akol and his cousins joined a large group of boys, all walking together. They were part of 20,000 young children with no adults to guide them, who traveled a long, long way—over 1,000 miles—to find safety. Their journey took them to a country called Ethiopia, but they couldn't stay there long because another war started there too.

So, they had to walk even further to another country called Kenya to a safe refugee camp that was called Kakuma. This camp was located in the hot desert and was home to many spiders, poisonous snakes, and scorpions, but Akol did not care because he was safe.

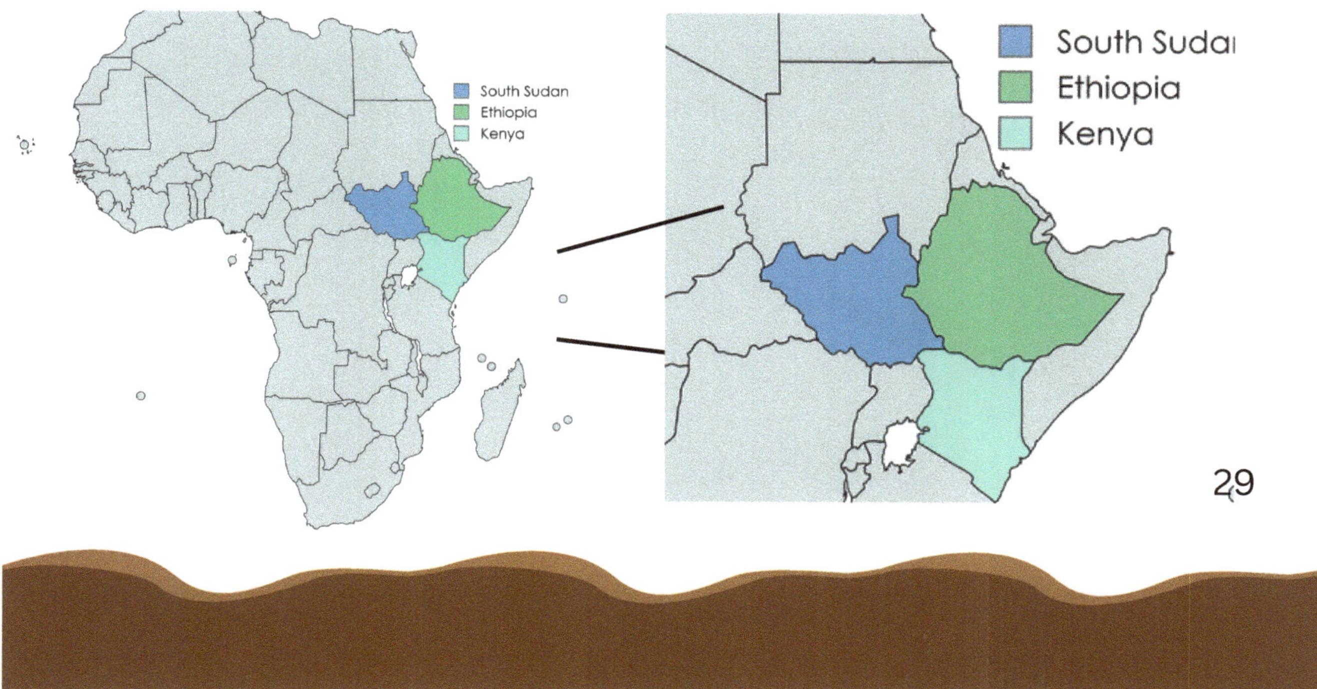

Akol and his friends lived in the Kakuma Camp for a few years. Then, something wonderful happened! The United Nations High Commission for Refugees helped Akol and some of his friends move to a new home far away in the United States. Akol was sent to live in a warm, sunny place called Jacksonville, Florida. He was a bit nervous in this new, big city, but he was also excited to make new friends and go to a special program just for kids like him called JaxTHRIVE.

Story 7

ZAINA'S CANDYLAND

A story from Iraq

In the heart of Baghdad, Zaina's grandfather "Gido," whom everyone loved, owned a special candy shop. Whenever anyone would enter, Gido would greet them with a big, warm smile. His shop was a colorful place filled with sweets that smelled as delicious as they looked.

As a small child, Zaina loved sitting on the counter, swinging her legs and looking at all the candies. Her favorite was the chocolate-covered caramels that would melt on her tongue! Gido would allow Zaina to try all the different candies, each one more exciting than the last!

32

But the best part about the candy store wasn't just the candies—it was the love and care Gido put into every little detail, making it a happy place for everyone who visited. Those sweet memories of Gido's store will always stay in Zaina's heart.

Zaina lived in Iraq until she was four years old, when the violence and constant bombings made life in her city too dangerous. Her father, whom she called Baba, was excellent at speaking English, and had worked for the U.S. Army as a translator. Because he was so helpful, her family got a special invitation to move to the United States, which people said was "a land full of opportunities."

They packed their bags, but not too many, because they didn't know what to expect. It was going to be an exciting adventure! They were sent to a city called Jacksonville, Florida, which would be their new home.

They were looking forward to all the opportunities and possibilities their new city would bring.

Soon after they arrived, Zaina's Mama learned about a fun program for kids like her called JaxTHRIVE. She was super excited and couldn't wait to go on Saturday to make new friends and study English, science and art. It was going to be another great adventure in her new life in America!

Zaina's favorite food is Dolma which are grape leaves with meat and spices. Young grapevine leaves are stuffed with a lemon-flavored mixture of rice, onion, and ground lamb.

JaxTHRIVE's Super Saturday Adventures!

Early Saturday morning, a cheerful bus makes its way toward JaxTHRIVE, a special place that welcomes refugee students in Jacksonville, Florida. The bus is filled with excitement and laughter as it approaches our "Super Saturday" program. The children race off the bus and are greeted by high-fives from the JaxTHRIVE volunteers, who have been eagerly waiting for their friends to arrive.

Ahmad is the first to jump out, waving hello with a huge smile, his cleats swinging over his shoulder! He heads straight to the science room, where Roya and Bilen are working with two JaxTHRIVE volunteers to conduct an experiment where ordinary household items are transformed into "elephant toothpaste"!

Their eyes open widely in discovery as this chemical reaction produces tubes of colorful foam that pours out of the top of a soda bottle. When they see Ahmad arrive, they invite him to join their group.

As Serhii finishes lacing up his cleats, he runs to the soccer field where other students are warming up. He teams up with Akol, who shouts to Amira and Ahmad, "Game on!"

In the art room, Galyna and Zaina whisper softly as they discuss their plans for the day's project: to paint their favorite memories from their home countries. They share treasured moments from Kyiv and Baghdad, thrilled to use the many art supplies, including colored pencils, paint, oil pastels, shiny sparkles, and many colorful decorations.

Once each group has visited all the Super Saturday learning stations, the students and volunteers head to the picnic tables for a healthy lunch and casual conversation. This is a chance for everyone to catch up and practice using American slang with the JaxTHRIVE volunteers. At 1:00pm we all clean up together before the bus comes to pick up the students and take them home.

JaxTHRIVE is powerful because it brings together students from all over the world into a safe and friendly environment. This helps heal their loneliness and makes them feel welcome. High school students from all over Jacksonville come to JaxTHRIVE to meet and make friends with refugee students who have settled in their city from many different countries.

When people of diverse backgrounds interact and make friends, everyone grows and benefits from the experience.

Acknowledgements

100% of the proceeds from this book and projects related to this book. will support resettled refugee students through our 501(c)(3) nonprofit organization JaxTHRIVE.

We sincerely thank all of our JaxTHRIVE volunteers and partners for supporting our mission and making a positive impact on our community.

We would also like to offer special thanks to Alexis Magnano, one of JaxTHRIVE's founders, for dedicating countless hours to assisting with the graphics, concepts, and storylines. Your hard work and creativity have been invaluable!

Finally, we would like to extend our heartfelt gratitude to our incredible students and their families for generously sharing glimpses of their lives back home. Their patience in answering our countless questions has been immensely appreciated. We thoroughly enjoyed learning about their lives and cultures, and we are truly thankful to have them as part of the JaxTHRIVE community.

To learn more about JaxTHRIVE or to get involved as a volunteer, please visit www.jaxthrive.org or email jaxthrive@gmail.com. To make a donation to support JaxTHRIVE's mission, please visit jaxthrive.org/donate."

References

"Child Displacement." UNICEF, June 2023,
https://data.unicef.org/topic/child-migration-and-
displacement/displacement/.

"Maps of Forcibly Displaced and Stateless People." UNHCR:
The UN Refugee Agency, https://www.unhcr.org/refugee-
statistics/annexes/forcibly-displaced-maps.html.

Refugee Statistics | USA for UNHCR.
https://www.unrefugees.org/refugee-facts/statistics/.

"What to know about refugee education and why it matters."
UNHCR: The UN Refugee Agency, 30 October 2023,
https://www.unrefugees.org/news/what-to-know-about-
refugee-education-and-why-it-
matters/#:~:text=Without%20the%20necessary%20investment
%20in,are%20not%20enrolled%20in%20school.

*Maps created using: https://www.mapchart.net/